Why Editors Drink

*A snarky look at common,
often hilarious, writing blunders*

Rob Reinalda

First edition

Published by Word Czar Media (www.WordCzarMedia.com), USA

ISBN: 978-1-09832-770-5

Book design: Teresa Reinalda
Illustrations: Teresa Reinalda
Cover photo: Casther/stock.adobe.com

Disclaimer: The examples and commentary in this book are
presented solely for the entertainment and edification of the
reader and are in no way intended to impugn the character or
professionalism of any individual, organization or other entity, public
or private.

For Teresa,
who gently encourages me to keep going, who laughs
in all the right places, and who makes the sun shine.

Introduction

Online writing can leave readers shaken, not stirred.

The Information Superhighway, as "they" dubbed the nascent internet, was supposed to bring a wealth of knowledge and insights within our reach. Extraordinary vistas awaited. Magnificent explorations of human ingenuity and intellectual pinnacles lay at our fingertips.

Then we screeched to a halt.

Before long, you see, everyone with a creaky pickup, a rusty hatchback with sketchy tires, or some other jalopy found that trundling up the digital on-ramp was as easy as securing a low-cost domain name.

Chaos ensued—enough to drive a person to drink.

Worst of all, though, was the business blog.

With no sense of direction, with blatant disregard for the rules of the road, and with no clue what the road signs meant nor how to use the brakes or the steering wheel, self-described "writers" galumphed onto the roadway, heedless of lane protocols. Their horns blared, and their flashers flashed—more for the sake of self-promotion than warning others. Still, wary wordsmiths who detected the hazards opted cannily to save themselves.

If they could, that is.

For some of us, the fate of intersecting with the verbally inept— the linguistic dawdlers, fast-lane weavers and no-signal left-turners—was unavoidable.

We were destined to take the path of greatest resistance: We became editors. It's rather like being a traffic cop in a demolition derby.

The accursed calling crept up on us, dawning at an early age. When Mrs. Pickering sought out volunteers to diagram a sentence, our hands shot skyward like rockets, drawing icy glares from our classmates.

Later, though, we became more utile than odious, as schoolmates sought us out, all smiles, entreating us to "just look this over" as they thrust incoherent essays our way and headed out for a night of pizza, while we stared with dilated pupils at the linguistic calamity before us, wondering where to start.

A few of our ilk were savvy enough to see the value of such labors and made sure to extract from their patrons a hefty sum for such overhauls. The rest of us went to work at newspapers.

My decades as a newspaper editor were extraordinarily rewarding. I worked with verbal virtuosi and relentless nitpickers, learning from both types and sharpening my natural acumen along the way.

The internet—which I'm sure you'll remember from the opening paragraphs—took a digital sledgehammer to print newspapers, which had survived pretty much everything else for centuries.

It took a while for news organizations to recalibrate and adapt, but they did. In the interim, tens of thousands of journalists bade farewell—one by one, or scores at a time— to the industry. (In the purge that tolled my departure, I walked out the door with two Pulitzer Prize winners, two of the bosses who'd hired me, and about 75 of our closest colleagues.)

Luckily, I was among the first to go. I found another editing position within months—on the day my erstwhile newspaper filed for bankruptcy. Soon after, the labor market was glutted with wordsmiths.

My new company—an online publisher—catered to communicators, and I learned that essays about writing did quite well in terms of traffic, so I wrote one. I don't recall the topic. I do recall the response: More, please.

Within months I had an audience. Soon I forged professional alliances, even partnerships, with extraordinary language experts. They helped me gain traction on social media, and on and on. I'm grateful.

As to the editing work, the curation process would funnel to my screen an array of articles from outside contributors displaying wildly disparate levels of competence. The difference from my newspaper days was striking.

Reporters are required to improve their writing skills, lest they be replaced by eager new faces who can readily distinguish a declension from a conjugation. For newspaper scribes, the message is clear: Get better, or get lost.

In the corporate world, people vary significantly in their desire to write and their aptitude for same. The general mandate is to churn out great quantity, not exceptional quality. That's a recipe for disaster.

My job and my mission were to improve the clarity and fluidity of the writing—or simply to distill the text to a few key points and pass those nuggets along to readers.

That would require, to varying degrees, a machete, a scalpel, pliers, a dental drill, a scythe, my gibberish-to-English dictionary, deep breaths, forceps, a potato peeler, an oft-tested sense of humor and the world's greatest invention: the Delete key.

What also helped, at day's end: a glass of pinot grigio. Maybe three.

I often joked with a fellow editor about the day's rigors and frustrations. On one occasion I offered a Post-it reading: "Pass the gin."

That phrase became shorthand for, "This week can't end soon enough." Some weeks it was uttered before lunchtime on Tuesday.

I applaud anyone who takes up a career in editing. Again, I was fortunate. Most of my co-workers—those who were truly my colleagues—were gracious and grateful. All are talented professionals.

Editing as a vocation engenders certain familiar laments.

A piece you reworked could be 65 percent yours, yet the byline—along with the credit for the well-crafted text— belongs to someone else.

In a given week, the same basic mistake might rear its ugly head in 20 different documents.

The quick turnaround you pull off to save the day might not get an acknowledgment of receipt, let alone a thank-you.

Then there are the mind-numbing, hand-wringing, head-shaking, jaw-dropping violations of common sense and the flagrant desecrations of linguistic protocols that prompt you to bellow a blue streak at the computer screen.

They fill this book, and they are why editors drink.

Grab a mug or stein, elegant stemware, a tumbler or a shot glass. We're going in.

Chapter 1

An aperitif

L ike the refreshing beverage served before a bounteous feast, here's a quick offering to whet your appetite—and your paring knife—before we venture into the banquet hall of business banalities.

As we embark, let's recall the words of the chain gang supervisor (Strother Martin) in "Cool Hand Luke":

"What we've got here is failure to communicate."

That's a common assertion among business writers. They bemoan the clutter, the lack of clarity, the stodginess of others' prose. They promise to impart to you The Secrets of Better Writing. Uh-huh.

They then blithely throw together such disparate elements as single-malt scotch and cream soda, or bloody mary mix and hazelnut liqueur. Sometimes the only remedy is to dump the swill, wash the glass thoroughly and start from scratch.

We're here not to vilify writers, but to highlight salient examples—with a jigger of rye humor, of course.

To that end, let's introduce Cedric Maunderton Blathersnoot. He'll be our scapegoat—the composite perpetrator of tautologies, mangled syntax, grammatical gaffes, reckless punctuation, verbal excesses and a host of other blunders.

Behold the following ladles of glop, a taste of things to come.

Cedric put the following iterations into the same article:

> *One of the most frequent problems I hear from fellow public relations professionals is that their leaders fail to communicate effectively.*
>
> *I've identified some of the most common reasons why leaders fail to communicate effectively.*

Wasting readers' time is a cardinal sin, so for their sake (and to bolster Cedric's bona fides as an effective communicator), let's reduce 35 words to 10:

> *PR pros say their bosses don't communicate well. Here's why.*

In that same article, Cedric has a lead-in and a sentence that immediately follows (and echoes) it:

> **They don't understand how important it is to communicate.** *Many leaders don't understand how important it is to communicate effectively.*

So, what you're saying is ...

> *An experiential marketing agency is taking a closer look at experiential marketing and asking - how can brands and agencies approach sustainability in their experiential marketing campaigns?*

Dammit, I thought this article was going to be about experiential marketing. What gives?

Pull up a bar stool. The first round's on me.

Chapter 2

Usage with a splash

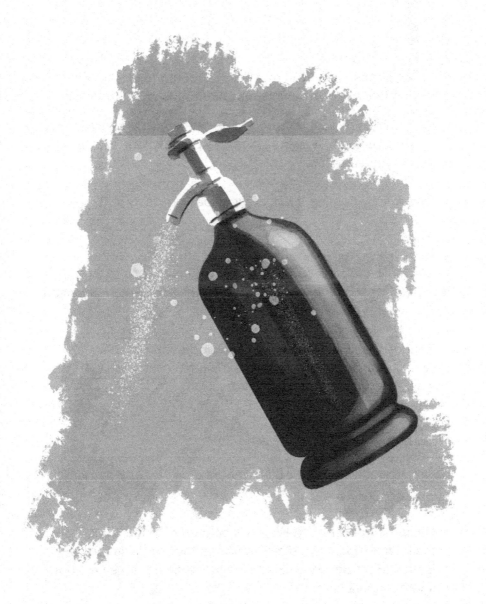

I n these examples, we'll see a recurring problem: Cedric doesn't give sufficient thought to words' meanings.

> *My goal for your content on LinkedIn is to get it to stick out like an eyesore when compared to any of those intrusive ads.*

I am quietly confident this author does precisely that.

> *Mention the sound-proof methodology your team used to create the content.*

Sound-proof? What's meant here, apparently, is either "sound" or "foolproof," which the writing clearly isn't. This is why editors reach for the 80 proof.

> *A little emoji marketing can go a long way, so be judicial with its use.*

Bang the gavel slowly. What's meant here is "judicious," meaning prudent. "Judicial" refers to the administration of justice. Both describe exercising judgment, but they are not interchangeable.

If only there were reference materials that explained the distinction ...

Looking stuff up used to require getting up, walking over to the dictionary, flipping through its pages (maybe puzzling over the whole alphabetical order thing), finding the word, and often cross-referencing it—consulting a different book, a thesaurus, to ensure you're using just the right term.

Now, you simply type a word or phrase into a search engine, and an array of options will pop up. With a few clicks, you can see words' definitions, etymology, synonyms, antonyms, Cinnabons, Auntie Em—yet people refuse to double-check for proper usage.

I'm not as much focused on quantifying the additional value add each delivers at the moment ...

Any tawny port in a storm such as that monsoon.

Beyond the jargony deployment of the verb "add" as a noun, Cedric pounds us with a mallet: "additional value add."

The whole sentence could be scrapped, because he's outlining what he's not doing—in first person, no less. (Yawn.)

For many years, one of the big mantras in PR has been that you should keep hammering away at the key messages you're trying to get across in a media interview, no matter what.

The term "mantra" is often applied to any maxim or slogan or motto, but it's loosely applied in such cases. Precise usage strengthens your writing and your credibility. In this case, such discernment would avoid insensitivity to those who take meditation seriously.

Consider these distinctions:

- Mantra: "Om mani padme hum."

- Maxim: "The customer is always right."

- Motto: "Be prepared."

- Slogan: "We do chicken right."

- Motto/slogan hybrid: "Be prepared—with 11 herbs and spices."

Selling something isn't as easy today than it used to be. Now we have a huge competition for every product and every service. Of course, in order to sell, you need to have a great product for people to want it. And, the most importantly, you need to tell them they want it. Doing this can be tricky. Often companies don't know the difference between a regular and a selling text. Average literary tricks that attract people in other kinds of texts wouldn't work here.

To be fair, English might not be the writer's primary language. That doesn't excuse a lack of editing, however.

There's no reason for a professional to publish a piece of writing without first having a knowledgeable colleague review it for clarity and proper usage. Otherwise you could end up, as above, with a verbal concoction resembling the "special punch" at the Grabba Cuppa Hoocha frat party.

Chapter 3

Grammar with a twist

G rammatical structure is the foundation of communication. Word order matters, as does delivering complete thoughts.

Increasingly common, however, is the arbitrary flouting of the rules—ostensibly demonstrating the writer's free-wheeling style—but doing so leaves the poor reader piecing together the various components and desperately trying to make sense of them. Here's a prime example:

> *We've all seen blog comments all but disappear. And social media conversations wane.*

I know it's considered absolutely adorable to begin sentences with conjunctions and that sentence fragments can be effective, but this sort of mangling of the rules serves no discernible purpose.

The above segmentation hinders readers' comprehension, and that's never a good result—except perhaps in surrealist theater and stream-of-consciousness novels. Ionesco and Faulkner have their audiences, but the cadre of business-to-business content consumers probably won't be among them, at least not during working hours.

The passage asserts that we've seen two things: "blog comments all but disappear" and "social media conversations wane." It's the same construction as, "We've all seen a dog and a cat." It would be silly to write it this way: "We've all seen a dog. And a cat."

So, let's write like adults (and I'll delete the clunky first "all"):

> *We've seen blog comments all but disappear and social media conversations wane.*

Sentence fragments work only when used sparingly. An olive in a martini is a nice embellishment, but no one wants to drink a glassful of olives.

> *Valentine's Day is right around the corner, and with it comes the usual pressure to get your loved one something that's just the right mix of romantic, thoughtful and personal.*

These are, of course, the days of verbs masquerading as nouns and other crossover linguistic identifications, but why not be clearer, especially when it's as easy as deleting a few words?

> *Valentine's Day is right around the corner, and with it comes the usual pressure to get your loved one something that's romantic, thoughtful and personal.*

Then there's the notion that conveying affection constitutes "pressure." If you truly love someone, don't you want to find ways to express that? Remember the words of Ogden Nash: "Candy is dandy, but liquor is quicker."

> *They're easy to scan, easy to digest, and lists are highly-shard content.*

Some sentences have multiple flaws requiring discrete

adjustments. Above, in addition to the false series, we have easily digested bits of glass: highly-shard content. (All too often, spell-check will let you down.)

So, anyway, what the heck is a "false series"?

That's my coinage for a disruption of parallel construction in a series. It is ubiquitous in spoken discourse and is creeping relentlessly into written text. Three or more elements in a series should be alike in form.

Here are a few fixes for the above:

> *They're easy to scan and easy to digest, and lists are highly shared content.*

> *Lists are easy to scan, easy to digest and easy to share.*

> *Lists are easy to scan, digest and share.*

> *... like a person's favorite color and birthday.*

My favorite birthday would be when I turned 17, I suppose, because then I could legally drive.

Yes, we know what's meant, but why not make it crystal clear:

> *... like a person's birthday and favorite color.*

Let's strive for clarity—paired with a flavorful claret.

Speaking of syntax:

> *Somehow, it's not only become common but accepted*

for the employee voice to be ignored.

Parallelism is important in the above construction, too.

What follows "but [also/even]" should match what follows "not only." The remedy in this instance is to transpose "not only" and "become":

> *Somehow, it's become not only common but accepted for the employee voice to be ignored.*

The revision ensures that "common" and "accepted" are equally weighted for the reader.

This one did <u>not</u> appear in a business blog, I will concede, but I so love its fractured syntax and vibrant imagery that I feel it warrants sharing.

> *I ask that you destroy that plastic shelving unit that mutilated me with an ax, please.*

By all means, avoid ax-wielding shelving units and all other potentially lethal home furnishings.

I do not offer a fix; its particular delight lies in its flagrant syntactic flaw. To the good friend who perpetrated this—and agreed to let me use it—I raise a toast with his favorite microbrew.

> *This means if you say you'll respond to emails the same day. Respond the same day.*

Some writers hack perfectly fine sentences into fragments, like so many Jonathan Brewsters cutting worms in half with their teeth. In this case, though, the sentences do not regenerate and become whole again.

No, they wriggle on as pathetic segments, causing readers to freeze in their tracks, horrified, bellowing, "For the love of Hannibal Lecter, what sort of fiend could have perpetrated such atrocities?"

The first sentence includes a dependent clause starting at "if," so for the meaning to come through, it must be constructed as a single sentence:

> *This means if you say you'll respond to emails the same day, respond the same day.*

Likewise, this next dark passage includes paragraphs containing sentence fragments that could be stitched together into a whole being. We'll dub them Frankengrafs.

Exhibits A and B are below:

> *So stop. And realize that when you "make an exception," to your rules and tell yourself it's because you are offering better client service, you are doing the opposite.*
>
> *You create an inconsistency. An action which doesn't align with the set-out expectation. By default, you set a new rule. So the client WON'T understand the next time you decide to follow the old one.*

You figure out that mess. I'll be at a wine tasting; it'll involve one bottle, but I'll keep tasting it.

More from that same source.

> *Be transparent in areas where the organization needs to improve.*
>
> *And do so in a solution-minded way.*

Cedric hacks up a perfectly fine compound sentence, and the severed limbs become <u>paragraphs</u>—of sorts. Keyboards should deliver little electrical zaps for such mutilations.

This is just fine:

> *Be transparent in areas where the organization needs to improve, and do so in a solution-minded way.*

This is even better:

> *Be transparent about areas requiring improvement, and keep solutions in mind.*

> *Tell powerful stories that stop us in our tracks and want to hear more.*

The stories want to hear more? I don't think so.

The problem here is twofold, so make mine a double. Beyond the flawed imagery lies a subtle contradiction: Do we want to be stopped, or to continue? Perhaps this would be clearer:

> *Tell powerful stories that make us want to hear more.*

I'll take a Manhattan <u>and</u> a Long Island iced tea. Cheers!

Chapter 4

Another round

H

ere's a look at repetition, redundancy, and still more redundantly repetitive iterations.

The way your home page looks visually ...

As opposed to how it looks olfactorily? In a similar vein:

Duplo, Lego's line of large-sized toys for toddlers ...

Large-sized, rather than large-flavored, one supposes. And:

Technology may someday give all the jobs to automated robots.

As a kid I had a cardboard "robot," which was <u>not</u> automated. He was an exception in the automaton realm. I daresay he would not have been a major player even in the unskilled labor market, much less a high-tech replacement kicking human employees to the professional curb.

After all, they're being asked about it already any way.

Got enough qualifiers in there, Cedric?

P.S. In that instance, "anyway" would be one word.

Let's try this, shall we?

They're already being asked about it.

Many marketers may be incredibly talented in a few of the traditional skills that have been around for a while.

Oh, <u>those</u> traditional skills. Glad to have that cleared up. I was figuring Cedric meant the traditional skills emerging daily, right along with the latest technologies.

One of those traditional skills (that have been around awhile, natch) would be reading the text and cutting tautologies.

Also, I trip over "traditional," which has a homespun connotation. To my mind, traditional skills would include needlepoint, pickling peppers, and stringing popcorn for the Christmas tree.

Know what? The whole thing is cumbersome; let's cut it by two-thirds:

> *Many marketers excel at certain time-honored professional skills.*

This next collection spotlights a common writing malady:

> **A gigantic list of tools for communicators**
> *So here you go...a gigantic list of tools we recommend.*

> **Be as concise as possible.** *Good leaders strive to remain as concise as possible. Speaking and writing concisely is all about conveying as much information as possible in the smallest possible space, which saves time and maximizes the effectiveness of your writing.*

Listen actively to every team member. *Finally, listen actively to every member of your team.*

Maybe it's something in the water. Then again, maybe it's something in the water.

That second blob is particularly appalling. After parroting the lead-in sentence, it contradicts the advice it purports to offer: Be concise.

Social media is always changing. And, 2017 will be no different.

Never mind the gratuitous "and" (with needless comma) at its outset; the second sentence adds nothing, so let's delete it. "Always" means always, so 2017 would be no different.

Social media is always changing.

Sticking with the calendar theme:

January is no longer the first month of an exciting year anymore.

Glad we have "anymore" in there, just in case readers glossed over "no longer." In a tangential vein:

While there is an astounding amount of back-and-forth and up-and-down wrangling about content, commas, and colors, this only occurs in May. Not all year long, as before.

Bewildered? So am I. It recalls comedian Lewis Black quoting a young woman as stating, apparently with abject sincerity, "If it weren't for my horse, I wouldn't have spent that year in college." (Maybe that makes horse sense.)

Deciphering the tangle of disparate elements requires dissection—and perhaps a mai tai or seven. Here we go:

> **While**
> *The author means "Although." Especially when there's a time element in the same sentence, it's best not to confuse readers with a two-way word. (Similarly, avoid "since" when you mean "because.")*
>
> **there is an astounding amount of**
> *I'll be the judge of what astounds me, thank you.*
>
> **back-and-forth and up-and-down wrangling**
> *This is distinct from to-and-fro and hither-and-yon wrangling, apparently.*
>
> **about content, commas, and colors,**
> *"I'll take 'Gratuitous Alliteration to Link Disparate Items' for $800, Alex."*
>
> **this**
> *Come on, Cedric. What "this" are you rambling on about now?*
>
> **only occurs in May.**
> *The word "only" should follow "occurs," as it modifies "in May."*
>
> **Not all year long, as before.**
> *Sentence fragments are enchanting—rather like a root canal.*

Tightening often clarifies:

> *The glut of wrangling about content, commas and colors occurs only in May—not all year long, as before.*

No, it still boggles the senses. Delete it, and let's move on.

Xxxxx Xxxxxxx, a PR Coordinator at Zzzzzzz Zzzzzzz, recommends that you pay special attention to the subject line. The details in your subject line play the most important role in determining whether the email will be opened or not. Make the subject line interesting enough to compel your target recipient to open it. The best subject lines are those that arrest the attention of readers. For example, if you are hosting a fundraising event over the weekend, the subject line could be something like; 'any weekend plans?'

OK, but what about the subject line? All kidding aside, five iterations are too many. Give your readers some credit, and let the context work for you.

Let's try this instead:

Xxxxx Xxxxxxx, a PR coordinator at Zzzzzzz Zzzzzzz, advises focusing on the subject line—notably on interesting details that grab recipients' attention and compel them to open your email. For example, if you're hosting a fundraiser Saturday, try, "Any weekend plans?"

Related twaddle:

Before opening an email, what is the first thing you look at? Although your answer was probably the name of the sender, the next thing you look at is the subject line. The subject line is the first thing that recipients see and it is what determines whether they will open the email or flag it as spam or even delete it without opening.

If a nifty subject line leads me to that swamp, I'll opt out. I have other things to do. After all, it's 5 o'clock somewhere.

Chapter 5

Blather, bloat chaser

M

any writers don't know how to get out of their own way.

> *Look at everything you thought you needed to say and instead share only 30 percent of what you were originally going to communicate.*

OK. Here you go:

> *Pare your original text by 70 percent.*

To that end, try to distill every sentence or phrase to its key point:

> *Learning new skills that work toward developing great communicators ...*

> *Learning pivotal communication skills ...*

I'm including this next paragraph in its entirety, because it reads like an editing test:

> *For many founders, PR is just a blip on the radar. But if you're looking to reach your audiences—because obviously—good media coverage can help speak*

to them. Clients and investors will hear your voice, and you can get your business to somewhere really awesome. And without further ado:

The above was offered as a preface to tips about securing media coverage through PR efforts—because obviously. It's <u>really awesome</u>.

Quicker and more effective would be:

PR helps secure media coverage, which reaches potential customers and investors alike. Here's how to get exposure for your clients:

That's 20 words, instead of 50, and now we know what's coming next and why.

As for "And without further ado," that's four words' worth of "further ado." Bid them adieu, and pour yourself a nice Bordeaux.

In the end, one of the most important things to remember is to make the best use of the resources you have: Your data, your content, your team, your customers, etc.

Of the first 18 words, 17 are needless. Only "use" is useful (as a verb).

Use the resources you have: your data, your content, your team, your customers, etc.

Better still, try this:

Optimize your data, content, team members, customers and other resources.

The word "optimize" is fine, used in moderation. Even tighter:

Optimize your resources: data, content, colleagues, customers, etc.

The biggest obstacle for many people is that they waste too much time seeking perfection.

Speaking of not wasting time, let's go with this condensed version:

Many people waste time seeking perfection.

Fifteen flabby words have been trimmed to the proverbial six-pack.

This is when our jobs as communicators combine with our roles as psychologists. Because communications IS about relationships. They are inseparable. And our relationship with our client or leadership drives our success.

Let's simply assemble those fragments into complete sentences.

This is when our jobs as communicators combine with our roles as psychologists, because communication is about relationships. They are inseparable, and our relationship with our client or leadership drives our success.

Better still, we'll help Cedric by tightening the text and tempering the self-endowed professional accreditation.

At times, the job of a communicator mimics that of a psychologist; communication is, after all, about relationships. Rapport with clients or leaders will drive our success.

If your content isn't getting the likes, shares or views you were hoping for, it's easy to blame a number of factors.

Perhaps you didn't get featured in the publication you were hoping to, or maybe the design wasn't right. These may be legitimate issues, but content flops are often because of one fundamental flaw: It didn't resonate with people.

That is throat-clearing on a bronchial level. There are 46 needless words leading up to the key point. Let's delete them.

Content flops are often because of one fundamental flaw: It didn't resonate with people.

I'd tighten it further:

Content flops when it doesn't resonate.

The tightening fixes the grammar and eliminates "with people." Could the content resonate with yaks, galoshes or zucchini? Not likely. In a live presentation the spoken content might resonate off the walls, but that scenario is not at issue here. Again, let the context work for you.

I've broken down examples of PR lessons derived

from several of my favorite cult classic movies that incorporate points all PR pros can leverage to benefit both their careers and their clients.

Cut it after "movies."

I've broken down examples of PR lessons derived from several of my favorite cult classic movies.

That way Cedric can convey the hackneyed premise in half the words.

Better still:

Here are PR lessons derived from some favorite cult classic movies.

Or even this:

Here are PR lessons derived from cult classics.

Readers need no more than that. We know from the byline exactly who did the deriving and whose favorites they are. We can easily glean from the rest of the article that the topic is movies.

Technology is often a driving factor of changing needs because it acts as a catalyst for change.

A catalyst, by definition, induces change. That makes three references to change in 17 words. Absent questioning the assertion itself—or seeking greater specificity—this boils it down:

Technology can change people's needs.

We all know that journalists are constantly bombarded with story ideas.

Let's consider several things here.

If "we all know" something, there's no point in stating the obvious, much less drawing attention to its obviousness.

Besides, if someone <u>doesn't</u> know X or disputes the assertion, you've insulted or otherwise annoyed that reader, which is not your best option.

That leaves the following:

Journalists are constantly bombarded with story ideas.

The word "bombarded" suggests relentlessness, so "constantly" can go.

Journalists are bombarded with story ideas.

That assertion warrants examination, notably the phrase "story ideas." How many of the pitches bombarding said journalists have any news value or even human interest? Damn few. The journalists might indeed be bombarded, but the merits of those incoming salvos would be hotly debated.

Speaking of stuff "we all know" ...

We all know that content is an important part of just about any marketing strategy, and it's especially important when it comes to your lead gen efforts. In fact, according to a recent study from Xxxxxx Xxxxx, nine out of every ten marketing agencies rate content marketing as a hugely successful part of their overall marketing mix. But content marketing can be an expensive undertaking, especially for small to mid-sized businesses operating on a limited budget. The good news? There are some exceptional, and exceptionally cost-effective tools you can use to help power your content marketing efforts. Let's take a look at a few of our team's favorite.

There it is, a large crate full of packing material, along with a teaser at the end to the real value—the "major award," if you will—to be delivered in the subsequent text. Here's a condensed version:

> *Strong content is essential in today's marketing, especially for lead generation. Content marketing can be expensive, but smaller companies on tight budgets can use the following cost-effective online tools.*

"What about that study the writer cited?" you might ask. A hyperlink in the opening phrase handles that. All other significant information appears in the 29-word revised text. (The original is 107 words.)

This is a Google Alerts alternative and I prefer it.

Simpler and stronger:

> *I prefer this Google Alerts alternative.*

This goes beyond bloat to an odd sort of anthropomorphism:

> *For example, if you're a real estate brokerage firm*

seeking to be quoted as an expert on the demand for office space in a certain market, data you can provide that illustrates the correlation between supply and demand, as well as clients/contacts who you can offer up to provide first-hand accounts of the challenge will help to frame your story and give the reporter more meat to work with.

Despite the infamous declaration, "Corporations are people, my friend," they're not; nor are "you" a real estate brokerage firm. You might wear a brick-patterned suit and comb your hair to look like slate roof shingles, but you're not fooling anyone—not even with that "doorbell" lapel pin.

Such behavior seems symptomatic of an edifice complex.

Here's a version trimmed from 69 to 47 words:

Let's say you work for a real estate brokerage and want to speak about the demand for office space in a certain market. Provide data on the supply/demand correlation, and offer clients and contacts who can provide relevant anecdotes. Those will frame your story and give the reporter substantial information.

All that reconstruction calls for a mint julep.

Here's an excerpt from a company statement:

This is a natural fit between two companies with great legacies of innovation that have shaped the modern media and communications landscape, and my senior management team and I are looking forward to working closely with Xxxxxxxx and our new colleagues as we begin to capture the tremendous opportunities this creates to make our content even more powerful, engaging and valuable for global audiences.

The above is not <u>structurally</u> problematic.

It is corporate maundering, however, and nobody wants to slog through it all. It reeks of mahogany paneling, freshly applied shoe polish and more than a whiff of halitosis.

Cut to the information chase and only include the essential stuff I simply must know.

Or, more succinctly:

Deliver only essential information.

Here's another example and its simple fix:

Be careful with the words you choose; keep all text short and to the point.

Choose words carefully; keep text concise.

Of note, dear readers: Over the years, I have made thousands of such corrections, whittling down authors' interminable exhortations about writing concisely. The preceding were just a handful.

Please enjoy a lovely cocktail; you've earned it.

Chapter 6

Up <u>and</u> on the rocks

Self-contradiction runs rampant, because — again — people smash words together like bumper cars.

> *Great media analysts develop an intuitive sense of what rings true...*

It seems to me intuition is innate, not a skill that one can develop.

> *We all know the proverb, "All work and no play makes Jack a dull boy."*
>
> *In 2016, that's no longer the case.*
>
> *Fewer than one-third of U.S. workers are engaged at work. Instead of coming to the office bursting with energy, many arrive dreading countless emails and meeting-packed afternoons.*

OK, so the proverb in the first paragraph warns against overwork. The second paragraph says that as of 2016, that caveat no longer applies. The third paragraph undercuts the refutation in the second paragraph.

Now the poor, pinballing reader has no idea what to think, except to go elsewhere to find something lucid to read — after downing a snifter of Armagnac to steady his or her frazzled nerves.

The easy solution: Eliminate the first two paragraphs, and start with "Fewer than ... "

There is a false presumption that more content means better results, when in reality that generally is never the case.

In "The Catcher in the Rye," J.D. Salinger brilliantly conveys imprecise teenage phrasing through his protagonist/narrator, Holden Caulfield, as in, "I always joke around like that sometimes."

In the above example, a professional writer offers a similar juxtaposition, with nary an iota of irony: "that generally is never the case." Cedric could have avoided the problem — and spared the reader some eye strain — by ending the sentence after "results."

There is a false presumption that more content means better results.

He might even recast it:

More content doesn't necessarily mean better results.

Always be available for conversation.
This is important for building morale within your team. You can't possibly be available for conversation 100 percent of the time, but you need to make your team

feel comfortable communicating with you.

Hold on. "Always" <u>means</u> "100 percent of the time."

That sort of muddle happens when a writer doesn't consider words' meanings—the downfall of much of today's writing.

"Always" is figurative, so Cedric should modify the guidance.

> **Be available to talk.**
> *To build team members' morale, try to be accessible, and keep exchanges as light and comfortable as possible.*

This can be scary but it should not scare or discourage you.

Wait ... what? The scary thing shouldn't scare you? Hmmmphh. Instead, the following conveys the idea without puffy contradiction:

> *That should not scare nor discourage you.*

Why change "this" to "that," by the way? As a rule, I use "that" for a point or element that came just before and "this" for the next thing to be presented or discussed. It's a shorthand that, used consistently, becomes a signal to the reader, like blinking the lights for last call.

I'm not going to say "a picture is worth a thousand words, so a video must be worth a million". You've likely heard that phrase before and rolled your eyes –

but what I will say is that video on social platforms is proven to generate great engagement.

For the love of Tom Collins, don't waste my time telling me you're not going to say something, saying it anyway, and then projecting my response to it.

Try serving it straight up, Cedric.

Video generates great engagement on social media platforms.

Clatter such as that original mess undermines the writer's credibility, seemingly in the name of a chummy, "personal" approach. It's treacle, and busy people don't have time for it. They have things to do, people to meet, places to go.

Speaking of which, one for the road, Joe.

Chapter 7

A dash of punctuation

T here's a capriciousness about the use and placement of punctuation marks, as though they are the stuff of whim or personal aesthetics. ("Oooh, here's a great spot for that dot-over-a-comma thingy.")

Why does it matter? Imagine using a question mark in place of a period. The following suggest disparate things:

"You're leaving?" versus "You're leaving." Beyond that: "You're leaving!"

Punctuation marks are road signs for readers, guiding them to your intended destination. Misuse these marks, and your audience will end up off your intended path—and reading someone else's stuff.

Imagine this drinking game: Every time someone inserted an apostrophe where it didn't belong, or whenever a comma was missing or misplaced, you'd take a shot of bourbon.

You'd be soused by the time you finished your commute— your <u>morning</u> commute, that is—just from reading signs outside businesses.

Similarly, many business writers neglect proper punctuation in their internal and external messages. That's confusing, and it can undermine readers' confidence in the writer's attention to detail.

When I speak—particularly when I do my three-hour CEO workshop—I offer a list of tools that everyone should at, the very least, check out.

Maybe that was simply mistyped, but how does that misplaced comma not get caught during, at the very least, a cursory proofreading?

We can use bold fonts to help point the audience toward certain words or concepts (see how Xxxxxxxx did that in the example above?).

The parenthetical is a full sentence, so it warrants being treated as such.

We can use bold fonts to help point the audience toward certain words or concepts. (See how Xxxxxxxx did that in the example above?)

Certain trends – such as Facebook's continued algorithm changes, the rise of virtual reality, live video and the continued rapid growth of Snapchat, are expected for 2017.

For the hell of it, Cedric tosses in an en dash, wrong for this purpose. Moreover, it's intended to set off the various trends, yet there's no closure to it (except for a comma after Snapchat, which doesn't work).

Here you go, Cedric (using em dashes):

Certain trends—such as Facebook's continued algorithm changes, the rise of virtual reality, live video and the continued rapid growth of Snapchat—are expected for 2017.

Or maybe this (with no dashes):

2017 is likely to see Facebook's continued algorithm changes, the rise of virtual reality, live video, and the continued rapid growth of Snapchat.

He's talking about amplification–highlighting–spotlighting.

Oh, goody, here are more arbitrary en dashes. Why confuse the reader with what might look like overachieving hyphens, given that commas would make better sense?

He's talking about amplification, highlighting, spotlighting.

To clarify, an en dash is most properly used to connect numerals, as in: catering to ages 15–22.

Today's writers overuse hyphens.

Employ hyphens in adjectival phrases (which modify nouns), but not in adverbial phrases (which modify verbs): "Let's have a face-to-face meeting," but, "Let's meet face to face."

Other phrases in which you should omit hyphens:

- **Call to action (and other multiword elements, such as power play)**
- **Independently verified (and other -ly adverbs, such as simply put)**
- **Log in to your account (as a verb)**

Remember, too, that a hyphen can change a meaning. For example, "re-creation" is different from "recreation."

One puzzlement for many writers is suspensive hyphenation. (No, that's not what is employed in the term "murder-mystery.")

Consider this sentence: The program is open to 13- to 17-year-old residents.

As with most other rules of punctuation, you can check by looking at what the words mean as they're connected or grouped.

Imagine that it read:

> *The program is open to 13-to-17-year old residents.*

That suggests that elderly residents who have lived there 13 to 17 years are the target demographic for the program. That's probably not the case. Yet the above mangling appears frequently, prompting the need for modification— and another little nipper of brandy.

> *They key here is not just to join one of these organizations–it's to raise your hand and volunteer. Might be uncomfortable at first, since you won't know a damn person. But, it'll get a lot easier as you go. Trust me–I've done this on more than one occasion and it's paid off every time.*

That passage is in this chapter for its punctuation missteps, but Cedric has afforded us multiple issues to address.

Here's that paragraph, amended. Compare and contrast.

> *The key here is not just to join one of these*

organizations; it's to raise your hand and volunteer. It might be uncomfortable at first, since you won't know a damn person, but it'll get a lot easier as you go. Trust me, I've done this on more than one occasion, and it's paid off every time.

I love semicolons; they turn comma splices into proper sentences and help you organize a complex series. Let's start with that first application:

> *PR is about elevating and sustaining brand reputation, marketing is about turning consumers at large into your customers.*

The preceding is a comma splice, a compound sentence comprising related clauses but lacking a conjunction to connect them.

Here's a simple fix, employing a semicolon:

> *PR is about elevating and sustaining brand reputation; marketing is about turning consumers at large into your customers.*

As in the above, the semicolon helps connect related yet distinct ideas.

Regarding the use of semicolons to distinguish smaller series within a larger series, consider the following:

> *I'm going to the hardware store for spackle, grout and wingnuts, the drugstore for lozenges, cuticle scissors and salve, and the green grocer for okra, kale and jicama.*

The reader might be able to sort that out as is, but let's make it a bit easier by deploying semicolons:

> *I'm going to the hardware store for spackle, grout and wingnuts; the drugstore for lozenges, cuticle scissors and salve; and the green grocer for okra, kale and jicama.*

What about the liquor store? That's a trip unto itself. In this profession, I need all available trunk space for that mission.

Mark Twain once denounced "whooping exclamation points," and F. Scott Fitzgerald advised a fellow writer, "An exclamation point is like laughing at your own joke."

Use them sparingly, if at all. If you feel your sentence needs one, find stronger words.

A discussion of commas could fill a book of its own. Those little hooks nestled at the bottom of a line of text can make a huge difference in a sentence's meaning. In some notable cases, the presence or absence of a comma has shifted a legal proceeding from one side's favor to the other's.

In this case, jurisprudence is not at issue, but clarity is:

> *Being truthful is better than being fraudulent and transparency is crucial for brand loyalty.*

A compound sentence—one with two subjects and two predicates—should have a comma before the conjunction (and, or, but). Therefore:

> *Being truthful is better than being fraudulent, and transparency is crucial for brand loyalty.*

Beyond the above adjustment, I'd go the extra step:

> *Being truthful and transparent is crucial for fostering brand loyalty.*

My goblet runneth over with editing.

As for apostrophes, their galling misuse is omnipresent.

They are properly used in contractions, standing in for extracted letters, for example: I'm, you're, she'll, it's (short for "it is"), they'd, weren't, and would've (a shortening of "would have," not "would of").

Likewise, they are used in shortening decades; placement is important. Note the following:

> *... installments of the series on the 90's Chicago Bulls.*

To abbreviate the 1990s, remember that you're removing the 19, so that's where the apostrophe goes: the '90s. Also, it's not a possessive, so omit the apostrophe between the 90 and the s.

> *... installments of the series on the '90s Chicago Bulls.*

Possessive apostrophes can cause confusion, because of shifts from singular to plural ownership, as well as variations among style guides—for example: Rhonda's anaconda, James' zither, the Crabtrees' 1928 Porter.

Even though an apostrophe comes into play with many possessives, such as those above, we do <u>not</u> write your's, their's, our's or it's (as a possessive form). Possessive pronouns do not take apostrophes.

It's a fairly simple rule to remember, especially compared with the genitive (possessive) case in German. (Trust me.)

You think those Oktoberfest mugs are enormous for the heck of it? No. It's because German grammar can be bewildering.

All that aside, German beer is *wunderbar. Prost!*

Chapter 8

A cocktail of missteps

Y ou've come this far. Take another shot of courage, and let's go on.

> *Why are so many organizations creating brand journalism platforms in the 21st century?*

Ummmmm, maybe because the 20th century is over and we'll all be dead by the time the 22nd century rolls around?

Excise gratuitous qualifiers.

> *If you're reading this article, you've already avoided making your first mistake as a digital marketer: not planning your first marketing campaign thoroughly.*

If you're <u>not</u> reading this article, please disregard.

Beyond that initial nonsense, there's a false premise: that reading the article equates to planning the campaign. The convergence of errors, the notion of avoidance and the multiple negatives only confound the poor reader.

Instead, Cedric, let's try this, put more positively and clearly:

> *Reading this article is a smart first step in planning your inaugural marketing campaign.*

What follows that assertion might be tremendous guidance

or utter pap, but the revision clarifies the author's objective.

Figuring out if you should jump in is possibly the trickiest step to overcome.

So, are we jumping or stepping, or perhaps leaping? Beyond that, should one have to <u>overcome</u> a step in a process?

You might hear such babbling from someone talking in her sleep after too many vodka stingers.

OK. Take a good, long swig before this next one.

Rinse, lather, repeat.

Really? Most people would have to <u>try</u> to screw up the all-too-familiar sequence: Lather. Rinse. Repeat.

Yet for Cedric, it's easy as cake, a piece of pie.

Seriously, why should I take business advice from someone who doesn't even know the proper order for shampooing? He'd be easy to spot, though. Just look for Mr. Sudsy Head.

Speaking of a sudsy head, this calls for a delicious weissbier.

Nobody wants to recall the famous scene from Ferris Bueller's Day Off when you are the one speaking. In fact, using that as a perfect example of what not do is spot on.

Where to begin? What the hell is Cedric talking about? Anyone? Anyone?

"Ferris Bueller's Day Off" includes easily a dozen "famous scenes"—among them Ferris (with friends in tow) catching a Cubs game at Wrigley Field, strolling through the Art Institute of Chicago, copping Abe Froman's restaurant reservation, or maybe lip-synching "Twist and Shout" on a parade float.

Yet the scene referenced (with Ben Stein as a teacher droning on about the Laffer Curve and "voodoo economics") pales against those gems.

As for deciphering the sentences themselves, one might as well be untangling wire hangers. The shift from third person to second person is jarring, but it's just a gateway to the subsequent jumble of ideas, which could send even the strictest teetotaler fleeing to the corner pub.

Don't force people to reread your text to glean the meaning.

It's hard to fathom that someone would commit those words, in that order, to writing. It also seems implausible that Cedric would put his name to them and hit "publish"—on a business blog to woo executive clients, no less. Yet there it is.

Let's try another approach to offering the same caveat.

> *A notable scene in "Ferris Bueller's Day Off" features Ben Stein as a teacher droning on about the Laffer Curve and "voodoo economics." Speakers should avoid that sort of soporific monotone.*

Or even this:

> *No speaker wants to be ignored like the droning economics teacher in "Ferris Bueller's Day Off."*

As a PR pro, I'm constantly trying to find learnings that I can relate to my everyday job, clients and colleagues (and let's be honest, correcting character's grammar).

One of those "learnings" ought to involve correct apostrophe placement in plural possessives.

Our office coordinator oversees this, typing up thank-you notes and wrapping them with chocolate pieces.

Wouldn't putting them into an envelope be easier and far less gooey? Maybe instead, *"including a few nicely wrapped pieces of chocolate."* Ensuring clarity warrants a few extra words.

Those liqueur-filled chocolate bottles might be a nice tribute.

While preventing a brand-damaging event can't always be avoided ...

That's right up there with, "I'll miss not seeing you."

Again, words have meanings, and those meanings augment or negate one another when used together. Funny, that.

In the chapter on usage, we talked about the importance of looking up words to verify their meaning, but fact-checking is important, too. Case in point:

In "The Elements of Style," by E.B. Strunk and William White ...

Someone wrote and published that—online, where people could see it.

I don't usually recommend guzzling tequila straight from the bottle, but it does lessen the sting of the 90 mph facepalm that doozy engenders.

Mobile devices are increasingly the way people (and, of course, employees) are getting their information.

The manatees using iPads, giant sequoias with Androids, and boxes of saltines texting furiously on their iPhones—all of whom make up a sizable part of any modern workforce—should not be overlooked.

If you don't see your employees as people, all the text messages in the world won't help. Here's a quick fix:

Mobile devices are increasingly the way people (notably your employees) are getting their information.

Better still, make people—not devices—the stars of an active-voice sentence.

More and more people (including your employees) get their information via mobile devices.

Not everyone who says they can do social media marketing have actually done it successfully!

Several things to fix: problems with subject/verb agreement, the needless "actually" and the annoying exclamation point.

Here are two alternatives to the original:

Social media marketing is easy to attempt but difficult to master.

Self-described social media marketers often fall short of success.

A well-delivered podcast, however, can keep its audience steadily engaged for up to an hour—perhaps even longer.

Ponder that for a moment: "up to an hour—perhaps even longer." The potential length of this stirring podcast, then, stretches from a nanosecond to eternity.

I imagine the boss saw very few results.

What if she saw only two results, and both were tremendously favorable?

Employees inboxes are packed.
We don't have to be communications experts to know employees inboxes are packed.

That hits the trifecta: repetition, bloat and faulty punctuation.

The last transgression is easiest to fix: employees' (possessive) inboxes.

The lead-in wording is repeated verbatim in the subsequent text. Cleverly, though, Cedric uses bloat to try to mask the repetition, stating something obvious not only to the target audience, but to any adult with a pulse. There is nothing of value in that second sentence.

On the upside, it's easily deleted.

> *Remember that adage about people judging a book by its cover? Well, now people aren't even opening the book; they're recommending it based on the jacket.*

Ummmm, the jacket <u>is</u> the cover—unless we're talking about paperbacks, which mimic the jacket of the hardcover version. Maybe Cedric was referring to e-books.

Wait.

Oh, hell.

From the same writer:

> *There isn't a fail-safe process, but there are some tricks.*

Fail-safe? Maybe Cedric meant "sound-proof."

Pass the gin.

Chapter 9

A dessert whine

T he exhortation to "write like you talk" was originally intended to steer writers away from stilted, jargon-laden claptrap in favor of something more universally accessible and digestible. Bravo to that.

As in many things, though, excess has created problems.

The resulting glide from corporate-speak toward a conversational tone picked up far too much momentum, and we've slid into slovenliness.

Think of it as shedding the three-piece, gray flannel suit and starched collar for business casual. Instead of stopping there—at sporting comfortable yet still professionally appropriate togs—we've careened to the point of showing up at the office in bunny slippers and mismatched (and not altogether fresh) pajamas.

We must find a balance. Writing can be more fluid without becoming sloppy, and it can remain professional and thoughtful without being stuffy and stilted.

It's time to reset the pendulum.

Let's start first thing in the morning; I'll have coffee, please, with milk, no sugar and no Irish whiskey.

-30-